NURSERY RHYMES

Illustrated by Jonathan Langley

PictureLions
An Imprint of HarperCollins*Publishers*

Nursery Rhymes is a selection of rhymes
and illustrations from the
Collins Book of Nursery Rhymes,
first published in hardback by
William Collins Sons and Co Ltd in 1990

Copyright text and illustrations
© William Collins Sons and Co Ltd 1981, 1990

This selection first published in Picture Lions in 1992
This edition first published in 1996
1 3 5 7 9 10 8 6 4 2
Picture Lions is an imprint of
the Children's Division, part of
HarperCollins Publishers Ltd,
77-85 Fulham Palace Road,
Hammersmith, London W6 8JB.
The author/illustrator asserts the moral right to be
identified as the author/illustrator of the work.
ISBN: 0 00 664133 4
All rights reserved.

Produced by HarperCollins Hong Kong.

CONTENTS

Baby Games 6

Mice Galore 8

Sing a Song of Sixpence 10

Nonsensical Rhymes 12

Mary Had a Little Lamb 14

Bad Boys and Naughty Girls 16

Jack and Jill 18

Lazy Days 20

Kings and Queens 22

Little Love Ditties 24

Are We Nearly There? 26

Here We Go Round the Mulberry Bush 28

Time for Bed... 30

Index of First Lines 32

Baby Games

This little piggy went to market;
This little piggy stayed at home;
This little piggy had roast beef;
This little piggy had none;
This little piggy cried, Wee, wee, wee,
  All the way home.

Tickly, tickly, on your knee,
If you laugh you don't love me.

Round and round the garden,
Like a teddy bear;
One step, two step,
Tickle you under there!

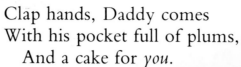

Clap hands, Daddy comes
With his pocket full of plums,
And a cake for *you*.

This is the way the ladies ride,
Nim, nim, nim, nim.
This is the way the gentlemen ride,
Trim, trim, trim, trim.
This is the way the farmers ride,
Trot, trot, trot, trot.
This is the way the huntsmen ride,
A-gallop, a-gallop, a-gallop.
This is the way the ploughboys ride,
Hobble-dy-hoy, hobble-dy-hoy.

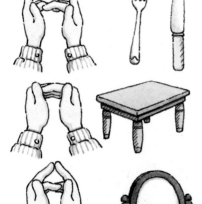

Here are the lady's knives and forks,
Here is the lady's table,
Here is the lady's looking-glass,
And here is the baby's cradle.

Mice Galore

Three blind mice, see how they run!
They all ran after the farmer's wife,
Who cut off their tails with a carving knife,
Did you ever see such a thing in your life,
    As three blind mice?

Three young rats with black felt hats,
Three young ducks with white straw flats,

Three young dogs with curling tails,
Three young cats with demi-veils,

Went out to walk with two young pigs
In satin vests and sorrel wigs;

But suddenly it chanced to rain
And so they all went home again.

Hickory, dickory, dock,
The mouse ran up the clock.
  The clock struck one,
  The mouse ran down,
Hickory, dickory, dock.

Six little mice sat down to spin;
Pussy passed by and she peeped in.
What are you doing, my little men?
Weaving coats for gentlemen.
Shall I come in and cut off your threads?
No, no, Mistress Pussy,
You'd bite off our heads.
Oh, no, I'll not; I'll help you to spin.
That may be so, but you can't come in.

Sing a Song of Sixpence

Sing a song of sixpence,
A pocket full of rye;
Four and twenty blackbirds,
Baked in a pie.

When the pie was opened,
The birds began to sing;
Wasn't that a dainty dish,
To set before the king?

The king was in his counting-house,
Counting out his money;
The queen was in the parlour,
Eating bread and honey.

The maid was in the garden,
Hanging out the clothes,
When down came a blackbird
And pecked off her nose.

Nonsensical Rhymes

Hey diddle, diddle,
The cat and the fiddle,
The cow jumped over the moon;
The little dog laughed
To see such sport,
And the dish ran away with
the spoon.

Hoddley, poddley, puddle and fogs,
Cats are to marry the poodle dogs;
Cats in blue jackets and dogs in red hats,
What will become of the mice and the rats?

Humpty Dumpty sat on a wall,
Humpty Dumpty had a great fall;
All the King's horses
And all the King's men
Couldn't put Humpty together again.

12

Rub-a-dub-dub,
Three men in a tub,
And how do you think they got there?
The butcher, the baker,
The candlestick-maker,
They all jumped out of a rotten potato,
'Twas enough to make a man stare.

Owen Moore went away,
Owing more than he could pay.
Owen Moore came back next day,
Owing more.

A man in the wilderness, he asked me,
How many strawberries grow in the sea?
I answered him, as I thought good,
As many red herrings as swim in the wood.

Mother, may I go out to swim?
    Yes, my darling daughter.
Hang your clothes on a hickory limb
    And don't go near the water.

13

Mary Had a Little Lamb

Mary had a little lamb,
  Its fleece was white as snow;
And everywhere that Mary went
  The lamb was sure to go.

It followed her to school one day,
  That was against the rule;
It made the children laugh and play
  To see a lamb at school.

And so the teacher turned it out,
But still it lingered near,
And waited patiently about
Till Mary did appear.

Why does the lamb love Mary so?
The eager children cry;
Why, Mary loves the lamb, you know,
The teacher did reply.

15

Bad Boys and Naughty Girls

Diddle, diddle, dumpling, my son John,
Went to bed with his trousers on;
One shoe off, and one shoe on,
Diddle, diddle, dumpling, my son John.

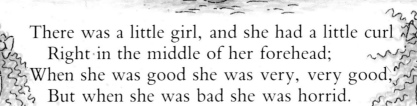

There was a little girl, and she had a little curl
Right in the middle of her forehead;
When she was good she was very, very good,
But when she was bad she was horrid.

Georgie Porgie, pudding and pie,
Kissed the girls and made them cry;
When the boys came out to play,
Georgie Porgie ran away.

Elsie Marley is grown so fine,
She won't get up to feed the swine,
But lies in bed till eight or nine.
Lazy Elsie Marley.

Little Tommy Tittlemouse
Lived in a little house;
He caught fishes
In other men's ditches.

Handy Pandy Jack-a-Dandy
Stole a piece of sugar candy
From the grocer's shoppy-shop,
And away did hoppy-hop.

Little Polly Flinders
Sat among the cinders,
Warming her pretty little toes;
Her mother came and caught her,
And whipped her little daughter
For spoiling her nice new clothes.

Jack and Jill

Jack and Jill
Went up the hill,
To fetch a pail of water;
Jack fell down,
And broke his crown,
And Jill came tumbling after.

Then up Jack got,
And home did trot,
As fast as he could caper;
He went to bed,
To mend his head,
With vinegar and brown paper.

Lazy Days

Buttercups and daisies,
Oh what pretty flowers
Coming in the springtime
To tell of sunny hours.
While the trees are leafless,
While the fields are bare,
Buttercups and daisies
Spring up everywhere.

A diller, a dollar,
A ten o'clock scholar,
What makes you come so soon?
You used to come at ten o'clock,
But now you come at noon.

Ladybird, ladybird,
Fly away home,
Your house is on fire
And your children are gone;
All except one
And that's little Ann
And she has crept under
The frying pan.

The cock's on the wood pile
Blowing his horn,
The bull's in the barn
A-threshing the corn,
The maids in the meadow
Are making the hay,
The ducks in the river
Are swimming away.

A swarm of bees in May
Is worth a load of hay;
A swarm of bees in June
Is worth a silver spoon;
A swarm of bees in July
Is not worth a fly.

Little Boy Blue,
Come blow your horn,
The sheep's in the meadow,
The cow's in the corn.
Where is the boy
Who looks after the sheep?
He's under a haycock
Fast asleep.
Will you wake him?
No, not I,
For if I do,
He's sure to cry.

Kings and Queens

Old King Cole
Was a merry old soul,
And a merry old soul was he;
He called for his pipe,
And he called for his bowl,
And he called for his fiddlers three.

Every fiddler he had a fiddle,
And a very fine fiddle had he
Oh, there's none so rare
As can compare
With King Cole and his fiddlers
three.

Hector Protector was dressed all in green;
Hector Protector was sent to the Queen.
The Queen did not like him,
No more did the King;
So Hector Protector was sent back again.

Lavender's blue, diddle, diddle,
Lavender's green;
When I am king, diddle, diddle,
You shall be queen.

I had a little nut tree,
Nothing would it bear
But a silver nutmeg
And a golden pear;
The king of Spain's daughter
Came to visit me,
And all for the sake
Of my little nut tree.
I skipped over water,
I danced over sea,
And all the birds in the air
Couldn't catch me.

The Queen of Hearts
She made some tarts,
All on a summer's day;
The Knave of Hearts
He stole those tarts,
And took them clean away.

The King of Hearts
Called for the tarts,
And beat the knave full sore;
The Knave of Hearts
Brought back the tarts,
And vowed he'd steal no more.

Little Love Ditties

Curly locks, Curly locks,
  Wilt thou be mine?
Thou shalt not wash dishes
  Nor yet feed the swine;
But sit on a cushion
  And sew a fine seam,
And feed upon strawberries,
  Sugar and cream.

What are little boys made of?
What are little boys made of?
  Frogs and snails
  And puppy-dogs' tails,
That's what little boys are made of.

What are little girls made of?
What are little girls made of?
  Sugar and spice
  And all things nice,
That's what little girls are made of.

One I love,
Two I love,
Three I love, I say,
Four I love with all my heart,
Five I cast away;
Six he loves me,
Seven he don't,
Eight we're lovers both;
Nine he comes,
Ten he tarries,
Eleven he courts,
Twelve he marries.

She loves me,
She loves me not,
She loves me,
She loves me not,
She loves me!

He loves me,
He don't,
He'll have me,
He won't
He would
If he could,
But he can't,
So he don't.

Roses are red,
Violets are blue,
Sugar is sweet
And so are you.

Are We Nearly There?

How many miles to Babylon?
Three-score and ten.
Can I get there by candle-light?
Yes, and back again.
If your heels are nimble and light,
You may get there by candle-light.

See-saw, sacradown,
Which is the way to London town?
One foot up and the other foot down,
That is the way to London town.

26

The man in the moon
Came down too soon,
And asked his way to Norwich;
He went by the south,
And burned his mouth
With sipping cold plum porridge.

Three wise men of Gotham
Went to sea in a bowl;
If the bowl had been stronger,
My tale would be longer.

Here we go round the mulberry bush,
The mulberry bush, the mulberry bush,
Here we go round the mulberry bush,
On a cold and frosty morning.

This is the way we wash our hands,
Wash our hands, wash our hands,
This is the way we wash our hands,
On a cold and frosty morning.

This is the way we wash our clothes,
Wash our clothes, wash our clothes,
This is the way we wash our clothes,
On a cold and frosty morning.

This is the way we go to school,
Go to school, go to school,
This is the way we go to school,
On a cold and frosty morning.

This is the way we come out of school,
Come out of school, come out of school,
This is the way we come out of school,
On a cold and frosty morning.

Boys and girls come out to play,
The moon doth shine as bright as day.
Leave your supper and leave your sleep,
And join your playfellows in the street.
Come with a whoop and come with a call,
Come with a good will or not at all.
Up the ladder and down the wall,
A half-penny loaf will serve us all;
You find milk, and I'll find flour,
And we'll have a pudding in half an hour.

Jack be nimble,
Jack be quick,
Jack jump over
The candlestick.

Twinkle, twinkle, little star,
How I wonder what you are!
Up above the world so high,
Like a diamond in the sky.

Wee Willie Winkie runs through the town,
Upstairs and downstairs in his night-gown,
Rapping at the window, crying through the lock,
Are all the children in their beds, it's now eight o'clock?

INDEX OF FIRST LINES

A diller, a dollar	20	Little Tommy Tittlemouse	17
A man in the wilderness, he asked me	13	Mary had a little lamb	14
A swarm of bees in May	21	Mother, may I go out to swim?	13
Boys and girls come out to play	30	Old King Cole	22
Buttercups and daisies	20	One I love, two I love	25
Clap hands, Daddy comes	7	Owen Moore went away	13
Curly locks, Curly locks	24	Roses are red	25
Diddle, diddle, dumpling, my son John	16	Round and round the garden	6
Elsie Marley is grown so fine	17	Rub-a-dub-dub	13
Georgie Porgie, pudding and pie	16	See-saw, sacradown	26
Handy Pandy Jack-a-Dandy	17	She loves me, she loves me not	25
Hector Protector was dressed all in green	22	Sing a song of sixpence	10
He loves me, he don't	25	Six little mice sat down to spin	9
Here are the lady's knives and forks	7	The cock's on the wood pile	21
Here we go round the mulberry bush	29	The man in the moon	27
Hey diddle, diddle	12	The Queen of Hearts	23
Hickory, dickory, dock	9	There was a little girl, and she had a little curl	16
Hoddley, poddley, puddle and fogs	12	This is the way the ladies ride	7
How many miles to Babylon?	26	This little piggy went to market	6
Humpty Dumpty sat on a wall	12	Three blind mice, see how they run!	8
I had a little nut tree	23	Three wise men of Gotham	27
Jack and Jill	18	Three young rats with black felt hats	8
Jack be nimble	31	Tickly, tickly, on your knee	6
Ladybird, ladybird	20	Twinkle, twinkle, little star	31
Lavender's blue, diddle, diddle	23	Wee Willie Winkie runs through the town	31
Little Boy Blue	21	What are little boys made of?	24
Little Polly Flinders	17